DK DORLING KINDERSLEY *READERS*

Level 1
Beginning to Read

A Day at Greenhill Farm
Truck Trouble
Tale of a Tadpole
Surprise Puppy!
Duckling Days
A Day at Seagull Beach
Whatever the Weather
Busy Buzzy Bee
Big Machines
Wild Baby Animals
LEGO: Trouble at the Bridge
A Bed for the Winter
Born to be a Butterfly

Level 2
Beginning to Read Alone

Dinosaur Dinners
Fire Fighter!
Bugs! Bugs! Bugs!
Slinky, Scaly Snakes!
Animal Hospital
The Little Ballerina
Munching, Crunching, Sniffing,
    and Snooping
The Secret Life of Trees
Winking, Blinking, Wiggling,
    and Waggling
Astronaut – Living in Space
LEGO: Castle Under Attack!
Twisters!
Holiday! Celebration Days around
    the World

Level 3
Reading Alone

Spacebusters
Beastly Tales
Shark Attack!
Titanic
Invaders from Outer Space
Movie Magic
Plants Bite Back!
Time Traveler
Bermuda Triangle
Tiger Tales
Aladdin
Heidi
LEGO: Mission to the Arctic
Zeppelin – The Age of
    the Airship
Spies

Level 4
Proficient Readers

Days of the Knights
Volcanoes
Secrets of the Mummies
Pirates!
Horse Heroes
Trojan Horse
Micromonsters
Going for Gold!
Extreme Machines
Flying Ace – The Story of
    Amelia Earhart
Robin Hood
Black Beauty
LEGO: Race for Survival
Free at Last! The Story of
    Martin Luther King, Jr.
Joan of Arc
Spooky Spinechillers

A Note to Parents

Dorling Kindersley Readers is a compelling new program for beginning readers, designed in conjunction with leading literacy experts, including Dr. Linda Gambrell, President of the National Reading Conference and past board member of the International Reading Association.

Beautiful illustrations and superb full-color photographs combine with engaging, easy-to-read stories to offer a fresh approach to each subject in the series. Each *Dorling Kindersley Reader* is guaranteed to capture a child's interest while developing his or her reading skills, general knowledge, and love of reading.

The four levels of *Dorling Kindersley Readers* are aimed at different reading abilities, enabling you to choose the books that are exactly right for your child:

Level 1 for **Preschool to Grade 1**
Level 2 for **Grades 1 to 3**
Level 3 for **Grades 2 and 3**
Level 4 for **Grades 2 to 4**

The "normal" age at which a child begins to read can be anywhere from three to eight years old, so these levels are intended only as a general guideline.

No matter which level you select, you can be sure that you are helping your child learn to read, then read to learn!

DK

A DORLING KINDERSLEY BOOK
www.dk.com

Project Editor Carey Combe
Senior Art Editor Diane Thistlethwaite

Senior Editor Linda Esposito
US Editor Regina Kahney
Production Melanie Dowland
Picture Researcher Kate Duncan
Illustrator Mike Bell

Reading Consultant
Linda Gambrell

First American Edition, 2000
2 4 6 8 10 9 7 5 3 1
Published in the United States by Dorling Kindersley Publishing, Inc.
95 Madison Avenue, New York, New York 10016

Published in Great Britain by Dorling Kindersley Limited.

Library of Congress Cataloging-in-Publication Data

Bull, Angela, 1936–
  Joan of Arc / by Angela Bull. -- 1st American ed.
    p.   cm. -- (Dorling Kindersley readers)
  Summary: A biography of the fifteenth-century peasant girl who led a
French army to victory against the English, witnessed the crowning of King
Charles VII, and was later burned at the stake for witchcraft.
  ISBN 0-7894-5718-0 (hc)--ISBN 0-7894-5719-9 (pbk.)
  1. Joan of Arc, Saint, 1412–1431--Juvenile literature. 2. Joan of Arc,
Saint, 1412–1431--Pictorial works--Juvenile literarture. 3. Christian women
saints--France--Biography--Juvenile works. 4. France--History--Charles VII,
1422–1461--Pictorial works--Juvenile literature. [1. Joan of Arc, Saint,
1422–1461. 2. Saints. 3. Women--Biography. 4. France--History--Charles VII,
1422–1461.] I.Title.II. Series.

DC103.5 .B84 2000
944'.026'092--dc21
  [B]   98-087251

Color reproduction by Colourscan, Singapore
Printed and bound in China by L.Rex Co., Ltd

The publisher would like to thank the following for their kind
permission to reproduce their photographs:
a=above; c=center; b=below; l=left; t=top
AKG London: Musée du Louvre: Jean Fouquet, photographer Erich
Lessing 14tl; Ulrich Molitor 22tl; **Ancient Art & Architecture Collection**:
8tl, 9cr, 32bl; Brian Wilson 9tr; J. Stevens 23br; R. Sheridan 15br;
The Art Archive: 4cl, 42tl; Musée Carnavalet 27r; St Roch Church 29tr;
Wernher Collection, Luton 5tr; **Bridgeman Art Library, London/New
York**: 11br, 15tr; 25, 34bl; English School 15th Century, Harley ms 6199,
f.57, Philip the Good (1396–1467) 30bl; National Gallery, London: Raffaello
Sanzio 6bl; National Portrait Gallery 28tl; Richardson and Kailas Icons,
London 6tl; **British Library, London**: 19cr; **Jean-Loup Charmet**: 41br;
Conseil General des Vosges: J. Laurencon 4tl; **DK Picture Library**: British
Museum 44bl, 45tr; Museum of London 11cr; Rye Town Hall 37tr; **Edimedia**:
27b, 38bl, 39b; **Mary Evans Picture Library**: 30t, 32tl, 38tl, 39tr, 46tl;
Chamoir 18tl; Lacroix 42bl; **Explorer**: P.Horvais 20–21, 37br; **Fotomas Index**:
22bl, 23t; **Photographie Giraudon**: 8cl, 36bl, 43tr, 44tl; Knudsens 40tl; Lauros
21cr, 35tr; **Sonia Halliday Photographs**: 24tl; **Robert Harding Picture
Library**: 7tr; **Kobal Collection**: 46bl; **Roger-viollet**: 16tl, 33tr, 34cl; **Scala**:
36tl; **David Simson**: 10cl; **Telegraph Colour Library**: Doug Corrance 47br.

Contents

JOAN OF ARC

Written by Angela Bull

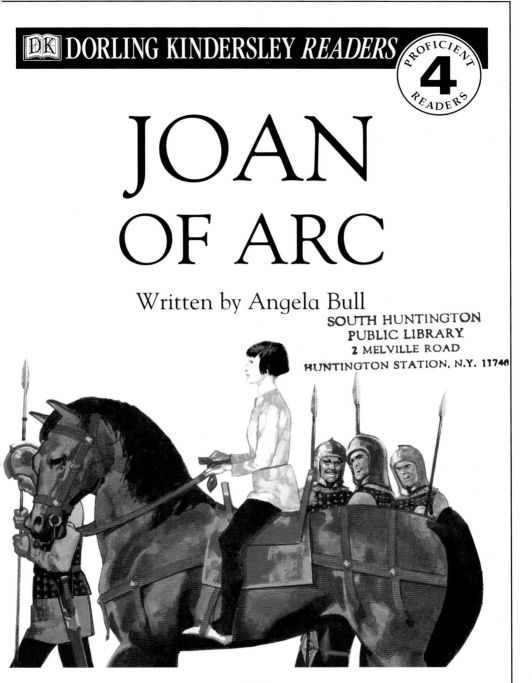

![DK]

DORLING KINDERSLEY PUBLISHING, INC.
www.dk.com

Joan's home
Joan lived in a small stone house similar to many others in the village. There was no running water or plumbing. Life was hard.

Agincourt
In 1415, the English beat the French in a famous battle at Agincourt in France. The English then went on to win more land.

Hearing voices

Joan of Arc was born in Domremy, a village in northeast France, in January 1412. It was a time of war. For 80 years French and English armies had clashed and, with the support of Burgundy, England now ruled northern France.

But Joan's family had nothing to do with the war. They were an ordinary village family. Her father was a farmer and her mother cared for the children. Joan was ordinary too. She didn't go to school, but she helped her mother and played with her friends. A favorite game was dancing around a special tree. Joan would hang flowers on its branches for the fairies.

One summer's day in 1424, Joan was playing outside with her friends.

"Your mother wants you, Joan!" a boy shouted. Joan quickly ran home, but found she wasn't needed.

Puzzled, she drifted into the garden. Suddenly, the local church bells rang out. Startled, she looked into the sky and saw a strange bright light. In the middle of the light stood an angel – Saint Michael.

Joan was terrified!

Then he spoke. "Be good, for God loves you." His kind voice soon melted all her fears away.

St. Michael
Michael was the fighting angel. The Bible said he defeated the devil (often shown as a dragon) when there was war in Heaven. People believed he helped Christian armies win wars.

Of Arc
In her lifetime, Joan herself never used a surname. People began writing "of Arc" to make Joan seem grander.

St. Margaret
Margaret was an early Christian girl. She wore men's clothes to join the monks of a monastery.

St. Catherine
Catherine was the best-loved saint of Joan's time. She was the patron saint of unmarried girls. Her body is buried near Domremy.

Over the next weeks two more saints, Catherine and Margaret, appeared to Joan. But she didn't tell anyone about them – she was afraid no one would believe her.

The saints changed Joan's life. She no longer played with her friends. Instead she went to church every day and, if she was outside when the bells rang, she dropped to her knees. The other children teased her for being too holy.

For five years the saints appeared – sometimes two or three times a day. They wore shining crowns and beautiful clothes and gave her wise advice in their kind, gentle voices. They were her friends – she loved and trusted them.

But gradually their messages darkened.

They told her there was dangerous work ahead that only she could carry out.

A horrified Joan listened as the saints told her she must help the French defeat the English.

"How can I?" she asked. "I am just a poor girl. I can't ride or fight like a soldier."

But her voices became louder and more and more persistent. Joan must save France!

Catherine wheel
St. Catherine converted 200 Roman soldiers to Christianity. When the Roman emperor discovered this, he was furious and condemned her to death. She was tied to a spiked wheel which spun around and killed her. The catherine wheel firework was named after her.

Women soldiers
In the Middle Ages only men could go to battle. Women were expected to stay at home. They were not allowed to become soldiers.

Charles VI
Charles VI, the Dauphin's father, became king at age 12. He went mad when he was 24. He howled like a wolf and hit his courtiers.

War in France
When men were away fighting, there was nobody to defend the women and children. Many were robbed and killed.

Message received

The turmoil in France was getting worse. Nobody knew who should be king. The English wanted their baby king, Henry VI, to have the throne. But the French had a prince, called the Dauphin (daw-FAN), whom they wanted to be crowned king.

Meanwhile, the country was falling apart. Crops were left in the fields as the men went off to fight. Hungry soldiers robbed anyone they came across. Children fought children from neighboring villages. The situation was desperate.

The saints continued to urge Joan on. But now they gave her exact instructions. First, she must defeat the English who had besieged Orleans. The town was surrounded by English soldiers and the people inside were starving as the English waited for them to surrender.

After she had beaten the English she was to ensure that the Dauphin was crowned king.

Nervous, but spurred on by her voices, Joan decided to visit a loyal French soldier, Robert de Baudricourt. She hoped he might help her. Bluntly, she told him that God wanted her to defeat the English and she needed his help.

Robert gazed down at the poor little village girl, with her long messy hair and her tattered clothes. Joan waited nervously for his response. Would he agree to help her?

Siege
Instead of wasting lives by attacking a well-defended town, armies used to wait outside until the people inside were so hungry they would give up without a fight.

No to marriage
When Joan was 16 her parents chose a man for her to marry. But she refused. This was brave, as girls most of the time either got married or became nuns.

9

To her distress, Robert laughed. She is talking nonsense, he thought. How could a young girl defeat the English? He soon sent her home.

Joan walked wearily back. She was very discouraged. How could she obey the saints now?

Months passed and the war seemed to be getting worse every day. Even her little village, Domremy, was attacked and burned to the ground. The villagers had to flee to a nearby walled town for safety.

Joan felt she must do something. With the saints encouraging her, Joan visited Robert once again.

This time Robert treated her with more respect. He was worried about the war and, as he looked at her again, he sensed something remarkable about her. She seemed so bold and so confident. Robert was impressed and decided to help her.

"Yes, all right. I'll do my best to help you," he promised. "I'll write to the Dauphin." Joan was thrilled.

Seals
A letter was folded up and sealed with a blob of wax. The sender would print his personal seal (often engraved on a ring) into the hot wax.

Post
There was no proper postal service. Messengers on horseback took the letters and could ride about 40 miles a day.

But Joan insisted that she visit the Dauphin personally. Robert soon relented and decided to send some of his soldiers to protect her on the long journey.

One young soldier he picked was John of Metz. John had never met a girl like Joan. There was no doubt in his mind that she was speaking the truth when she said, "There is no help for the kingdom but in me."

But the soldiers were worried. How would she travel in safety? Joan already had her answer – the saints had given it to her. "As a boy," she said.

Taking off her dress, she put on a pair of black trousers, a boy's tunic, and boots. She then had her long hair cut short. Astride her horse for the first time, she felt strange – half a girl and half a boy. "Call me Joan the Maid," she told her companions.

Together they set off on their long, dangerous journey to Chinon, where the Dauphin was staying. They rode all day and often had to sleep on the ground at night.

In a village called Fierbois, they found a small shrine dedicated to St. Catherine. Overjoyed, Joan knelt and prayed for her saint's blessing. Renewed in her belief, she rode on.

Joan the Maid
"The Maid" was the name Joan gave herself. It meant a girl who was too young to marry. By using this name Joan showed that she didn't think she was grown-up. She also hoped it would keep her safe.

The Dauphin

Charles the Dauphin, son of the last French king, was staying at the castle of Chinon – well away from the battlefields. He was not a brave young man. He had done nothing to help his people. He had just waited, hoping things would get better by themselves.

Joan and her companions reached his castle on February 24, 1429. After a night's sleep, she was summoned to see the Dauphin.

The Dauphin had got Robert's letter, so he knew why she'd come. But he thought her story about the saints was so unlikely that he decided to test her with a trick. He ordered that Joan must pick him out from among a large crowd of elegant courtiers at his court.

Spoiled prince
The Dauphin was spoiled and had led a sheltered childhood. He was always borrowing money from courtiers to buy himself treats.

Castle rooms
Most castle bedrooms had bare stone walls, rushes on the floor, and a small fireplace to keep it warm. The bed was surrounded by curtains for extra warmth.

Joan didn't hesitate. Prompted by her voices, she walked straight up to a young man with a bulging nose and drooping eyelids. She quickly knelt before him.

"You are the Dauphin," she announced.

She had correctly identified the Dauphin. In that instant he began to believe that Joan had been sent by God. He listened eagerly as she told him how she would defeat the English army and see him crowned king at Rheims.

It sounded like a wonderful plan!

French courtier
Courtiers wore long velvet robes, trimmed with fur for warmth.

This stained-glass window shows Joan finding the Dauphin from among a crowd of courtiers.

Armor
Over a shirt of chainmail or leather, knights wore a metal breastplate fastened with leather straps. The knights also had metal covers for their legs, arms, and even hands.

Joan's servants
Joan had two servants to look after her things and cook for her, two pages to wait on her, and two heralds who carried messages around for her.

But the Dauphin was cautious. Thrilled though he was, he decided to give Joan a further test. He sent her to some churchmen who questioned her about the voices she was hearing. But Joan's simple faith impressed even them, and they advised the Dauphin to trust her.

Swinging from doubt to certainty, the Dauphin suddenly couldn't do enough for her. He promised that she would lead the French army against the English at Orleans. He showered her with splendid armor, a magnificent white horse, and enough servants for a knight. She needed a banner to carry into battle, he said. So she chose a plain white one decorated with God blessing the emblem of France – the lily.

But when the Dauphin gave her a sword, Joan refused it. She said that her voices had told her of a sword at St. Catherine's shrine at Fierbois.

A servant was immediately sent to look for the sword. To everyone's amazement, a magnificent sword was found exactly where Joan said it would be. It was caked in rust which, the instant it was picked up, crumbled away, leaving a glorious, gleaming sword.

Now Joan was ready for battle.

Orleans siege
The English had 11 forts outside the city walls. But there was still a route into the city, so the city was not yet starving. There was not much fighting – the English and French generals even gave each other presents!

Orleans

Joan's first battle was to be at Orleans. The city stood on the Loire River where English and French lands met. If the English captured it, nothing would prevent them from marching into the heart of France. It was up to Joan to stop them.

Around Orleans stood a ring of English forts filled with soldiers. They had been there for six months waiting for the French to surrender. But there was still one way into the city – a small gate in the eastern wall. Joan decided to head for it.

Riding her white horse and carrying her striking banner, Joan approached Orleans. Puzzled but excited, the army followed her.

Suddenly they stopped. The wide Loire River lay between them and the city. The only way to cross the river was by boat, but the wind was blowing in the wrong direction.

"God will help us!" shouted an excited Joan.

Suddenly, to the amazement of the soldiers, the wind changed direction – they quickly crossed the river. As Joan led them into Orleans, the townspeople went wild. At last they might be saved. But fierce battles still lay ahead.

Boats
Sailing boats were the quickest way to cross. But the French army used whatever boats were available, such as fishing boats and ferries.

English army
English property owners had to supply soldiers according to how rich they were. For instance, in 1429, someone worth $15 (a lot of money in those days) had to send one mounted spearman!

Battleaxe

Joan carried a small battleaxe with her. It had a lethal metal spike and a small blade that could pierce armor.

Sword

These were often about four feet long with sharp edges along both sides. A short sword, or dagger, was used for hand-to-hand combat.

Mace

A mace was a very heavy wooden club that had a metal end covered in sharp spikes. Maces were used to break bones and dig into flesh.

Joan decided on an all-out attack against the English. Her plan horrified her cautious French officers – but it worked! Waving her banner and calling on God to help her, Joan and her excited soldiers charged against the English forts.

The French fought bravely and fearlessly and the English army soon crumbled, surrendering fort after fort.

Joan wore no helmet and never drew her sword during the battle, for she dreaded killing anyone. But her presence inspired the soldiers to fight harder, until only the strongest fort remained in English hands.

"You'll be wounded," her voices warned her. But Joan didn't care – the final victory was too close. She dashed toward the last fort.

But suddenly she felt a stab of pain – an arrow had hit her in the shoulder.

Showing great courage, Joan pulled it out and rushed back to the fight. Seeing her safe, the French troops battled on until the English gave way. Abandoning everything, the English army fled from Orleans.

It was a great victory for the French. At last the English enemies were on the run – and it was all because of Joan the Maid.

Longbow
Longbows were six feet long and were used to fire arrows at horsemen. The crossbow was smaller.

Cannon
Cannons fired stone balls at the town walls to try and make holes in them.

Catapult
Catapults were used to hurl huge rocks – or sometimes dead animals to spread disease.

Joan having her wound dressed after her victory at Orleans.

The Coronation

The English were bitter about their defeat. Their general complained that they had been beaten by witchcraft. But the French believed that Joan was truly inspired by God.

The Dauphin was delighted with Joan's spectacular victory. But when she told him that her voices wanted him to go to Rheims to be crowned king, the cowardly Dauphin refused. Rheims was in northern France – enemy territory. He wasn't eager to go there!

Joan had no doubts. Her voices had commanded it – and all French kings were crowned at Rheims. To prove she could get the Dauphin there safely, she undertook a series of battles against nearby towns held by the English. Once again she was successful. The mere sight of this girl struck terror into the English army.

Witchcraft
Everyone believed in witches in the Middle Ages. Witches were thought to cast spells that caused illness and madness.

Ducking
One way of discovering if someone was a witch was to duck her in water. If she drowned she was innocent!

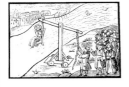

Scaling ladders
Soldiers attacking a walled town carried ladders with hooks, which hooked over the wall. They would try to rush up the ladder before it was pushed over from above.

Rheims
From 1180 on, the kings of France were always crowned at Rheims cathedral. This was because the holy oil was kept there.

Town after town fell. Once, as she led the way up a scaling ladder, a stone knocked her to the ground but she fought on, undaunted.

Faced with Joan's many triumphs, the faint-hearted Dauphin saw that he had no choice. Reluctantly he agreed to go with her to Rheims to be crowned king.

Stained glass
Medieval stained glass windows were made of small pieces of colored glass held together with lead. Since people couldn't read and didn't have bibles, the pictures in these intricate glass windows told stories of Christian faith.

Coronation rites
No one could rightly be called the king of France until he had been crowned at Rheims and marked with a touch of the holy oil.

Despite the Dauphin's concerns, the long journey to Rheims proved easy. Towns that were ruled by the English and Burgundians opened their gates and let Joan and the Dauphin pass through along with their soldiers and noblemen.

As they approached Rheims, swarms of white butterflies clustered around Joan's banner. Proudly, she led the Dauphin into the city. People poured into the streets to cheer the arrival of their future king.

Arrangements to crown the Dauphin were made at top speed. The coronation took place the next day in Rheims' beautiful cathedral, under huge stained-glass windows.

Decked in golden robes, even the ugly little Dauphin looked splendid. And by his side stood Joan, resplendent in her shining armor and carrying her white banner.

25

Soldiers
Life for ordinary 15th-century soldiers could be very tough. They slept on the ground, they often had to steal their food, and there were no doctors so they had to tend to their own wounds.

Too thin
Joan very rarely ate and was very thin. Today this would be called anorexia. Joan may have wanted to appear thin so that she would look more like a boy.

How life had changed for Joan! Six months earlier she'd been an ordinary village girl. Now, dressed like an important knight, she was responsible for a king's coronation.

However, as the royal procession left the cathedral to be greeted by excited crowds, Joan had a dreadful feeling that everything was over. But how could it be? Half of France, including Paris, the capital, was still in English hands. Joan was desperate to go on fighting until all her kingdom was free.

And it wasn't just for France – it was also for herself. She really loved her new life, dressing in boys' clothes and mingling with all the soldiers.

To keep fit she'd almost stopped eating and she no longer had periods like a normal girl. But it didn't matter to Joan as long as she could go on leading the triumphant French army. Eagerly, she asked the king for permission to recapture Paris.

King Charles was horrified. He didn't like war. And when his enemies suggested a truce, in which they could keep Paris, he was pleased to agree. Dismissing Joan, he quickly traveled back south to resume his old idle life.

Origins of Paris
Paris was named after an ancient tribe, the Parisii, who had first lived there. It became France's capital in 508 A.D.

Paris
Paris was first built on an island in the Seine River – the I'lle de la Cité – now in the middle of modern Paris. In Joan's time Paris had expanded along both banks of the river, but the city was well guarded with high walls surrounding it.

The king leading his courtiers in to his castle

27

Henry V
In 1415 King Henry V of England invaded France and managed to conquer all of northern France, including the capital, Paris. With the help of Burgundy, he was a successful and powerful ruler. Henry died in 1422.

War wounds
With no doctors and very basic medicine, most soldiers died from wounds they received on the battlefield.

Things go wrong

Despite the king's lack of interest, Joan wasn't giving up. She was determined to recapture Paris. But in her eagerness to fight she had forgotten her voices. The saints hadn't asked her to go on – they were silent. But Joan didn't notice.

She threw herself eagerly into preparations for a new attack. There were plenty of soldiers still willing to follow her and she gathered them together at St. Denis, a small town outside Paris. From here she planned to attack the capital.

Right from the start the battle went badly. A makeshift bridge, over which she hoped to cross the Seine River into Paris, was burned on the secret orders of the king. Cheated and furious, Joan fought on. But when she was seriously wounded in the thigh, she and her soldiers were forced to give up the struggle.

Joan was bitterly disappointed – it was her first defeat in battle.

Then she realized the date. She'd been fighting on September 8, the birthday of the Virgin Mary and a very holy day. No wonder God and the saints hadn't helped her! Full of remorse, she hung up her armor in the abbey of St. Denis.

St. Denis
St. Denis, the patron saint of France, was the first Christian bishop of Paris. The abbey of St. Denis was where French kings were buried.

Holy mother
The Catholic Church celebrates many special days connected with the Virgin Mary, the mother of Jesus.

Entertainment

At court, during the evening meal, minstrels would entertain the guests, singing and playing on lutes, harps, drums, and trumpets. When there was no music, people told amazing stories.

Burgundy

Burgundy was a huge area in eastern France ruled by a very powerful family. The area slowly became more detached from France, and the two kingdoms often fought each other over land and power.

The coronation had not turned the Dauphin into a great warrior king. He was still the same cowardly little man who liked singing and dancing better than battles. Despite England and Burgundy still holding northern France, the king disbanded the army. He claimed that he'd made a truce with England and that he couldn't pay his soldiers. Joan was horrified.

Although Joan's wound had eventually healed, she felt miserable and restless. She was haunted by the fact that her saints had told her that she only had one year to save France. Time was quickly running out.

Without the king's permission, Joan gathered together some unemployed soldiers and began attacking enemy towns. It felt good to be back in action again and the soldiers followed her willingly. But she started getting beaten more often. In one battle she broke the sword that had been found at St. Catherine's shrine. Worst of all, her saints' voices were silent.

With dismay, Joan realized that she could no longer always do the miraculous things that she, and others, expected of her.

Herbal medicine
Medicine of the time was based on superstition rather than science. Herbs were used for everything and treatment was basic. Lungwort was used for chest disorders, feverfew was generally used for headaches, and wormwood was placed in clothing to repel fleas.

feverfew

lungwort

wormwood

Marching
A soldier wore leather boots laced at the front. They could be worn on either foot and had no hard soles for protection on rough ground – but a soldier's feet grew tough with marching.

Ramparts
These tall embankments surrounding a fort were the first line of its defenses.

In the spring of 1430, Joan moved north to fight. For a short time it seemed that things might go better. She marched on a town called Melun and its people threw out their Burgundian rulers and surrendered at the mere sight of her.

That evening, as Joan looked down from the ramparts of the captured town, she felt very happy.

Suddenly St. Margaret and St. Catherine appeared. However, they had nothing kind or encouraging to say. Instead, they warned her bluntly that she would soon be captured.

But nothing would put Joan off her mission to defeat the English.

Ahead of her lay Compiègne. It was in French hands but some Burgundian soldiers were ready to take

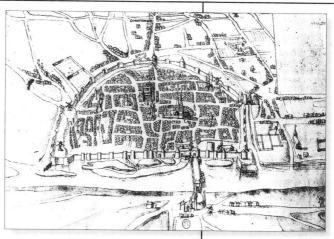

it. Joan hurried there to help.

The next day she rode out with her soldiers to attack the besiegers. But they were much stronger than she expected and her soldiers fled.

Joan was left entirely alone – surrounded by the enemy.

Compiègne
The small town of Compiègne was of strategic importance to the English as it lay directly on their supply route from England.

Allies
Burgundy was helping the English because the French king and the Duke of Burgundy both wanted to rule France. Burgundy hoped that with the help of the English, the French king would be unseated.

Rich ladies wore beautiful dresses.

Prisoner

Suddenly a Burgundian soldier grabbed the golden coat Joan wore over her armor and pulled her off her horse. As the saints had predicted, she was captured by the enemy.

When news of Joan's capture became known, people from all over France begged the king to pay the ransom demanded to release Joan. But King Charles stubbornly refused.

Although Joan had helped him to be crowned, he'd had enough of her going on about war. He wasn't willing to pay a single franc for her. Instead, the English offered 10,000 francs, and Joan was given to them.

The English imprisoned her in a strong castle tower. Ladies living in the castle were shocked by the boys' clothes Joan wore. They offered her a dress to wear, but she refused.

"God hasn't given me permission to change clothes," she said.

Despite her refusal, the ladies were kind to her. Knowing that she hated being confined, they let her walk on the castle battlements. As Joan walked she thought of her bleak future. The English would want revenge for their defeats and were bound to be cruel. She shivered as she peered over the edge of the tower. Could she escape?

Gathering all her courage, Joan jumped from the sixty-foot wall.

Prisons
Prisons were mainly used as places to hold people awaiting trial. Prison terms were not given as punishments. The usual punishments were fines or mutilations.

God
In Joan's time everyone believed in God. Leaders in war were desperate to persuade their citizens that God was on their side.

Hell
To be beaten in war meant that God was not on your side and therefore you would be sent to hell, a dreadful place of eternal fire.

Joan crashed to the courtyard below. She was stunned but unhurt. Instantly, guards surrounded her and dragged her back to a cell. Her desperate escape attempt had failed.

Meanwhile, her English captors plotted her downfall. They had many reasons for hating Joan. First she had humiliated them at Orleans, then she'd made the dauphin king of France, instead of their king. And, though they claimed she'd used witchcraft, they feared that if she did drive them out of France it might prove that God was against them. That was unbearable!

They needed to prove that Joan was the enemy of God. So they decided to charge her with witchcraft and heresy, claiming that Joan believed she knew better than the Church. The punishment for both was death – an outcome that would suit them well!

Still in her boys' clothes, Joan was moved to a prison at Rouen, a center of English power in France. Here she was tightly shackled with a chain around her feet, and guarded day and night by mocking soldiers. Joan became very depressed.

But she had one comfort. Her voices began speaking to her again in their old reassuring way.

Postcard showing Rouen tower

26. ROUEN
Tour - Musée Jeanne d'Arc
Tower - Joan of Arc Museum

Reste du Château fort bâti par Philippe-Auguste en 1207.
Jeanne d'Arc prisonnière (24 Mai 1430) y fut enfermée; elle y comparut devant ses Juges

Justice
Even though Joan was tried in a French church court, all the priests and clerics there supported the English.

Judge Cauchon
Cauchon, the bishop of Beauvais, was a clever, hard-headed man. Though he was French, he was an important member of the English king's council.

The trial

Alone and frightened, Joan perched on a small footstool. In front of her sat nearly 200 men, staring at her with cold eyes. These men were to act as her judge and jury – she was very scared.

Joan was in the Great Justice Hall at Rouen. She had no one to defend her. All she had were her quick wits, the courage she'd always shown in battle, and the belief that she'd done nothing wrong.

Then the questions started. She tried to answer truthfully and boldly, as her voices had told her to do. Even when the questions were hostile or confusing – particularly so from Judge Cauchon, the man in charge – she stood her ground.

From the start Cauchon attacked her about the boys' clothes she wore – church laws forbade women to do so.

"Why do you insist on dressing like a boy?" asked Cauchon repeatedly. Joan explained that it was for her safety. While living with male soldiers, it was better not to be thought of as a woman. Wearing male clothes helped to protect her.

"Besides," said Joan, "my voices commanded it."

Church laws
Joan's judges quoted a verse in the Bible that said: "A woman must not wear men's clothing." Joan had broken this commandment.

Clothes' rules
French laws about who could wear which clothes were very strict. Only noblewomen could wear fabrics such as brocade, velvet, and rich cloth embroidered with silver or gold thread.

Joan defending herself against a jury of clergymen.

But it was Joan's voices that caused her the most trouble. Her hostile English questioners refused to believe in them. Why, they asked, would saints speak to an ignorant little French girl? Clearly, they said, the voices must have come from the devil and, if she talked to devils, Joan herself must be a witch.

Joan argued her case boldly. She insisted her voices were heavenly, as they brought her courage and comfort. Enraged by Joan's stubbornness, Judge Cauchon assured her she was wrong.

"The Church understands these false voices much better than you do," said Cauchon.

Joan wouldn't agree. In most matters she trusted the Church's judgment, she said, but in this her own experience counted for more.

In the Middle Ages prisoners were often tortured to make them "confess" to crimes. They might be stretched on the rack, or be chained upright with their neck in an iron collar, or have their feet squashed in iron boots.

The judges were infuriated by her stubbornness. To frighten her, they led her to a torture chamber. Here, among the horrific screws, spikes, and racks, they threatened to torture her unless she accepted the Church's view. Despite her fear of being tortured, Joan refused. She was ill, exhausted, and frightened, but she wouldn't give way in her beliefs.

People were stabbed when the door shut.

41

Burning
When someone was found guilty of heresy they were always burned to death.

Execution
Upper-class criminals were beheaded with a sword or an axe and their heads stuck on city gates. Lower-class people were hanged and their bodies were left up to rot.

Finally, Joan was taken to a cemetery. There, right in front of her, was a stake for burning people. Joan was told that unless she admitted she was wrong, she would be burned to death.

Terrified at the prospect, a weeping Joan finally gave in.

"I was mistaken!" Joan cried. "My voices are from the devil."

A paper with her confession already written on it was thrust before her. Unable to write, she signed with a shaky "O." Now, she thought, she would be set free.

Instead, she was solemnly told that, although she was to be spared the burning, her punishment was lifelong imprisonment.

Devastated, Joan was dragged back to her cell, where her hair was shaved off and she was forced to wear a dress.

Joan was frantic. Not only must she stay chained in prison, but she'd denied her voices. They spoke to her then, telling her how wrong she had been. Joan couldn't bear it.

Knowing it meant death, she tore off the dress and pulled on the boys' clothes that had been left in the cell.

Her saints wanted her to be honest to herself and to them – she would have to face the fire.

Punishment
The Church had a few prisons for heretics who changed their mind (known as recanting). They would be shut up for life in tiny dark cells and would be given nothing but bread and water for the rest of their lives.

Mass
The Mass is the central act of the Christian Church. Bread and wine are given to the worshippers to remind them of Jesus's last supper. They believe that by taking Mass they are in touch with God's presence.

Cross
Joan believed, as everyone did, that Jesus had died for her on the cross. The little cross helped remind her that Jesus was with her as she suffered.

Hearing what she'd done, Judge Cauchon visited Joan's cell. In tears she told him that she'd only signed the confession out of fear – she still believed her voices were from God. Cauchon sentenced her to burn.

On May 30, 1431, Joan heard Mass for the last time. She wore a dress dipped in sulfur, which would burn quickly. A dunce's cap, labeling her a heretic and a witch, was stuck on her shaven head, and she was taken to the marketplace.

More than ten thousand people stood to watch her die. The crowd was silent as she was tied to the stake. A kind English soldier gave her a cross made of two sticks – Joan tucked it in her dress.

The brush fire was lit. Quickly, it roared upwards. In agony, Joan cried out to her saints.

As flames and smoke hid her from the silent crowd, her voice was still heard crying: "Jesus! Jesus!"

Then there was silence. Choked by fumes, scorched by fire, Joan's life came to an abrupt end.

She was only nineteen years old.

Joan's ashes
Christians collected relics of saints and holy people. By throwing the ashes into the river, the executioner made sure that there was nothing left of Joan for future worshippers.

The end

There was no cheering as Joan died. The crowds felt terrible – even the English. "We've burned a saint," one soldier groaned.

After Joan's death the English began to lose heart. They weren't so sure of their right to be in France. Under continued attack they retreated north until, eventually, all their French lands were lost.

Orleans never forgot the girl who had ended their siege. Neither did King Charles. Even though he had refused to ransom Joan, he felt very guilty when he heard of her death.

After France had recaptured the town of Rouen, he sent for a copy of the trial. Charles was horrified to see how unfair it was. He quickly ordered a retrial. Many people who knew and loved Joan gave evidence. This time Joan was completely cleared of witchcraft and heresy.

Sainthood
Saints were especially close to God in life and are believed to stay close to Him in Heaven. Prayers can be said to saints to ask for help.

Joan in films
There have been a number of successful films and plays about Joan. In 1923, just after she was made a saint, writer George Bernard Shaw wrote a play about her.

In 1920, the Pope decreed that Joan was a saint. Now there are statues of her all over France. Pictures have been painted of her, and books, plays, and even films written about her.

The girl who died to save her country will never be forgotten.

Remembrance
Joan is remembered throughout France. Orleans has a huge statue of her. Rouen cathedral has a chapel dedicated to her and there is a chapel where she was burned.

Statue of Joan at Orleans

Glossary

Abbey
A large church where monks live and work.

Armor
Protective body covering, made mainly of metal, and worn for fighting.

Banner
A flag with a person's special emblem on it.

Battlements
The walls around the top of a castle. There are narrow indentations in the wall through which arrows or a cannon could be fired.

Confession
An admission, often to a priest, of wrong things done or said.

Coronation
A special ceremony in which a new king or queen is crowned.

Courtiers
Lords and ladies who lived at the royal court as companions and attendants for members of the royal family.

Dauphin
The title of the heir to the French throne.

Dukedom
An area of land, like Burgundy, ruled by a duke, an important nobleman.

Dunce's cap
A tall hat that is put on people who are considered stupid.

Faith
Complete belief and trust in something or someone.

Fort
A small, well-defended tower or castle in which soldiers can live safely.

Franc
The money used in France.

Heresy
A belief which is different from the established beliefs of the Church.

Retrial
A second trial held when the verdict of a first trial has been challenged.

Saint
A person who has been recognized by the Church as especially holy.

Shackles
Metal chains which secure prisoners around the wrists or ankles to stop them from escaping.

Shrine
A holy place, usually a church, associated with a particular saint.

Stake
A tall, strong stick placed upright in a fire, to which the victim is tied.

Sulfur
A yellow acid which burns quickly.

Surrender
To voluntarily stop fighting and give up to your enemy.

Truce
An agreement between enemies to stop fighting.

Virgin Mary
The mother of Jesus Christ, and so a person of special holiness

Voices
The messages Joan heard which she believed came from the saints. They probably spoke inside her head rather than aloud.

Witchcraft
The power of practicing magic, often for evil purposes.

Index

jB
JOAN

Bull, Angela.

Joan of Arc.

$12.95

DATE			